GW00976190

Kingfisher Books, Grisewood & Dempsey Ltd,
Elsley House, 24-30 Great Titchfield Street,
London W1P 7AD

First published in 1993 by Kingfisher Books
2 4 6 8 10 9 7 5 3

Material in this edition was previously published by
Kingfisher Books in *On the Move: Truck* in 1990.

© Grisewood & Dempsey Ltd 1990, 1993

British Library Cataloguing in Publication Data
A catalogue record for this book is available from
the British Library
ISBN 1 85697 090 6

Series editor: Veronica Pennycook
Series designer: Terry Woodley
Typeset in 3B2
Phototypeset by SPAN
Printed in Great Britain by
BPCC Paulton Books Limited

The Big Truck

Angela Royston
Illustrated by John Farman

Kingfisher Books

In this book

The truck in this story is an articulated truck. It has two parts, a tractor at the front and a trailer behind.

Trailer

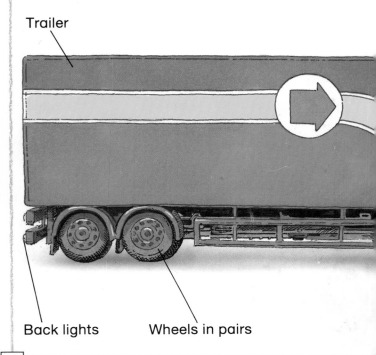

Back lights   Wheels in pairs

The driver's cab is in the tractor. The trailer is like a huge box on wheels which is hooked up to the tractor and pulled along. Goods are loaded into the trailer and are often driven a long distance to be delivered.

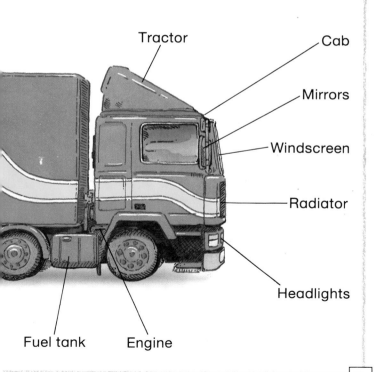

Tractor

Cab

Mirrors

Windscreen

Radiator

Headlights

Fuel tank

Engine

Sam arrives for work

It is a cold, wet morning and the big truck is parked in the corner of the truck depot. Sam pulls on his cap and walks across the busy yard to his truck.

Today Sam is taking his truck to the docks to deliver a load of medicines.

He checks there is enough water in the radiator and enough oil in the engine. Then he climbs into the cab and drives over to the fuel pump to fill up with fuel.

Driving in the rain

Sam drives through the streets to the motorway. He changes gear as the heavy truck slowly picks up speed. It's raining but the big windscreen and mirrors give him a good view of the motorway in front and behind.

Sam turns off the motorway.
The road he takes to the docks is
narrow and a car is parked on the
corner where the truck has to turn.

First the tractor then the trailer
turns, but the wheels along one
side scrape the pavement.

At the docks

A ship has just come into the docks and is being unloaded. Sam drives over to a huge warehouse. He puts on the brakes and they hiss loudly.

He climbs down and goes to the office with his delivery papers.

A forklift truck takes the crates of medicine off the trailer. Then some big bales of cloth are lifted in. Sam is going to take this new load to a cloth warehouse in another city.

A flat tyre

Sam has a long journey ahead, but as he drives out of the docks he realizes that something is wrong with one of the wheels. He pulls into a layby and gets out to check. One of the tyres is flat.

"Oh no!" he groans. "Must have torn it getting round that tight corner!" Using his mobile phone, Sam asks for a mechanic to come and help him. Then he gets out his lunch-box and settles down in the cab to wait.

Help arrives

Just as Sam is beginning to wonder if he'll have to wait all day, he sees the mechanic's van pull into the layby. Sam shows him the damaged wheel.

"We'll have you back on the road in no time," says Martin the mechanic, as he gets his tool box out of the van.

First he lifts the wheel off the ground with a jack. Then he uses an airgun to undo the nuts that hold the wheel in place.

Changing the tyre

Martin takes off the flat tyre.
Sam pulls the huge spare wheel
out from under the tractor and
rolls it over to him. Together they
lift it into place.

"Soon be finished now," says
Martin. While Martin is tightening
the wheel nuts, Sam puts the flat
tyre away.

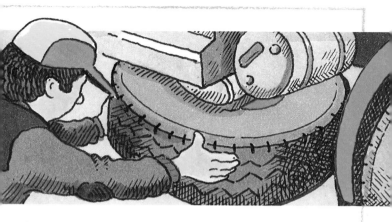

The job is done. Sam thanks Martin for helping him and then climbs up into his cab. He wants to get on with his journey without losing any more time.

Before setting off again, Sam phones the cloth warehouse to let them know he's had a delay. They warn him to drive carefully because a snowstorm has been forecast for later.

A night in the cab

Sam drives on for a few hours, until it starts to get dark. Then he uses his CB radio to find out what other truck drivers know about the road ahead. They say that the snow has started so Sam decides to stop at the next transport cafe.

He eats in the cafe and then goes back to his cab to sleep. At the back of the cab is a cosy bunk bed. Sam climbs in and pulls the curtains together. He sets his alarm clock so it will wake him early in the morning, ready for another day's driving.

Snow chains

During the night the snow falls heavily. Sam knows the mountain roads ahead will be slippery, so he unhooks the trailer and fits snow chains around the tractor

wheels to help them grip the road better. Later that morning he sees a long traffic jam on the other side of the road. A large truck has got stuck climbing a steep hill. "They'll be there for hours," thinks Sam. "I'm glad I put the chains on."

A tight squeeze

That afternoon Sam finally arrives at the warehouse where he is to deliver the cloth. "Park over there," says Hugh the foreman. Sam looks at the narrow space between two other trucks.

He has to shunt backwards and forwards, slowly moving the trailer into the right position. At last Hugh shouts "OK!" and Sam turns off the engine with a sigh of relief. Then Hugh checks the load and signs the delivery papers.

The next load

Sam unhooks the trailer from the tractor. It will be unloaded later and vans will deliver the cloth to several shops. Hugh shows Sam another trailer. "This one has to go to the airport," he says. Sam backs the tractor slowly up to it.

The back of the tractor connects with a large pin on the trailer and the two lock together. Sam climbs out and links up the cables for the brakes and lights.

"Just the fuel and oil to check and then I'll be off again," he says to Hugh.

Some special words

Airgun   A machine that works like a spanner, loosening and tightening nuts on bolts.

CB radio   Citizens' Band radio. Truck drivers can talk to each other on CB radio.

Depot   A yard with warehouses and offices where trucks collect and deliver goods.

Gears   A part of the engine that helps to control the car or truck's speed.

Layby   A place at the side of the road where cars and trucks can pull over and stop.

Index

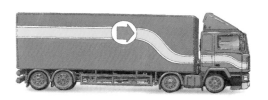